Dr Fact's
Planets of the Solar System

This book belongs to

Dedicated to every child,
in every corner of
planet Earth.
You have a special part to play
in making
the world better. 😊

First published in 2022

ISBN 9798767158454

DR ADEBOLA ADISA

b e i n s p i r e d

Dr Fact's Series 1 Book 2

Dr Fact's
Planets of the Solar System

Written by Dr Adebola Adisa   Illustrated by Srgimini

"The heavens tell the glory of God.
And the skies announce what his hands
have made."

-Psalm 19 vs 1 ICB

Dr Fact: Hello, I am Dr Fact.

Erin: Hello, I am Erin.

Mo: Hello, I am Mo.

Dr Fact: It's good to see you again, Erin and Mo.

Erin: It's good to be back, Dr Fact.

Mo: Yes, it is good to be back.

Dr Fact: It's facts time children.

Erin and Mo: Yay!

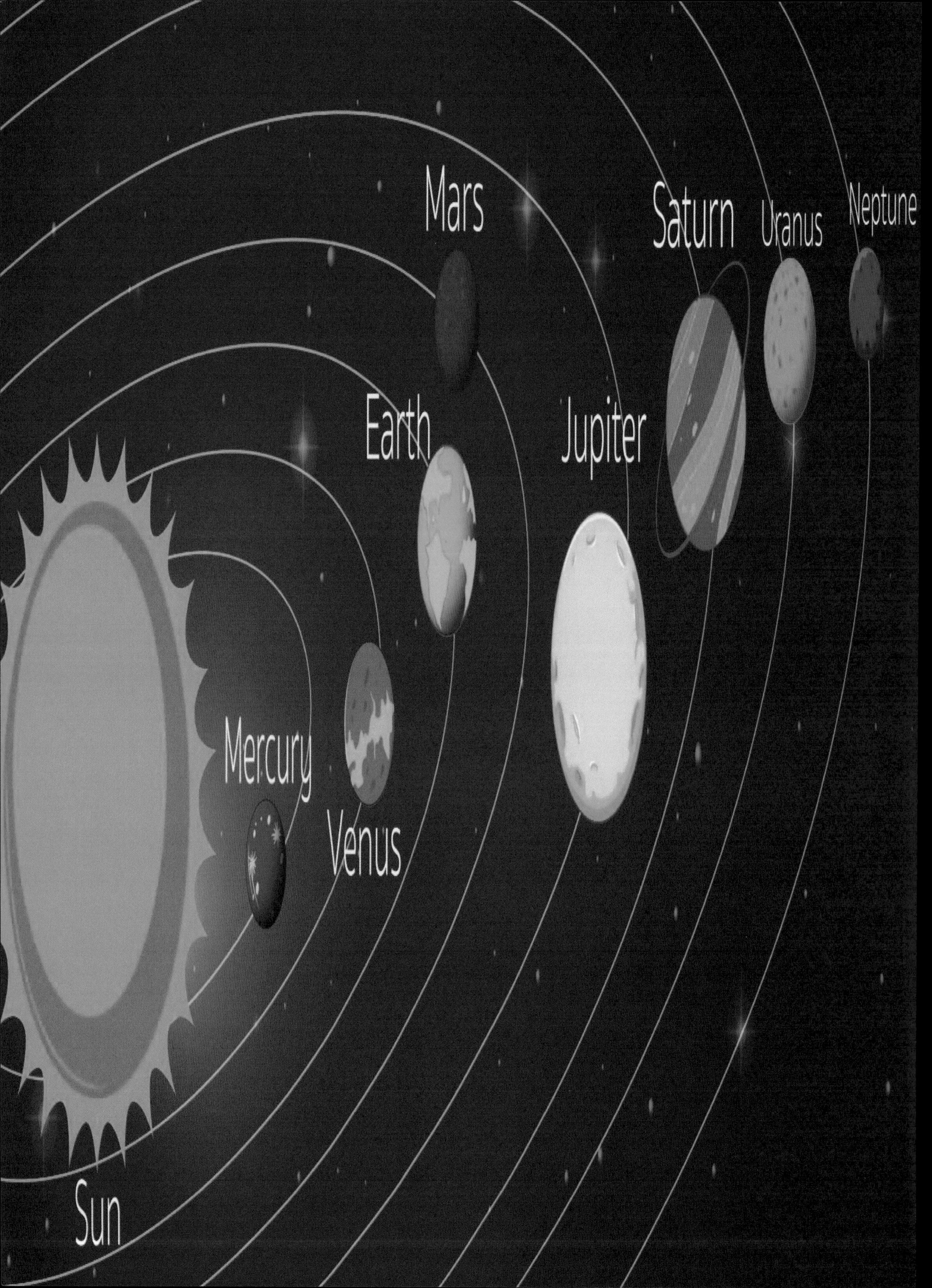

Mars

Saturn

Uranus

Neptune

Earth

Jupiter

Mercury

Venus

Sun

Dr Fact: *Our planetary system is the solar system.*

The Latin word for the Sun is "solis", and anything related to the Sun is solar.

Erin: *Can you tell us more, Dr Fact?*

Dr Fact: *The solar system consists of: the Sun, and everything bound to it by gravity; the planets, dwarf planets, dozens of moons, millions of asteroids, comets, and meteoroids.*

MERCURY

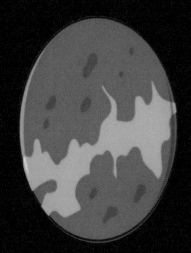

VENUS

Earth

MARS

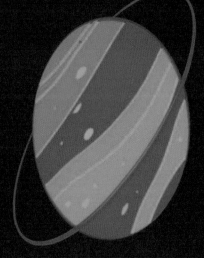

SATURN

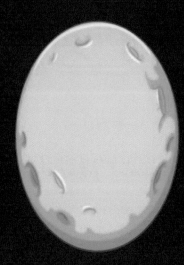

JUPITER

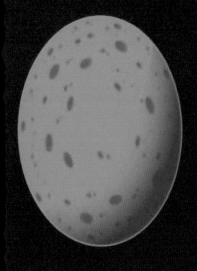

URANUS

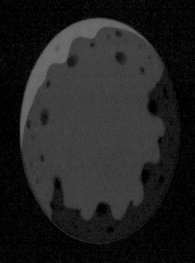

NEPTUNE

Mo: What are planets?

Dr Fact: Planets are large natural bodies that travel around stars. There are eight solar planets. These are: Mercury, Venus, Earth, Mars, Jupiter, Saturn, Uranus, and Neptune. Four of them: Mercury, Venus, Earth, and Mars are known as the rocky planets.

Erin and Mo: Wow!

Dr Fact: Now, let me tell you more about the planets in the solar system.

Mercury

MERCURY

Mercury is the smallest planet in the solar system, and the closest to the Sun.

It has a thin atmosphere called Exosphere.

Mercury is also the fastest planet in the solar system.

The closer a planet is to the Sun, the faster it is because it has a shorter distance to travel.

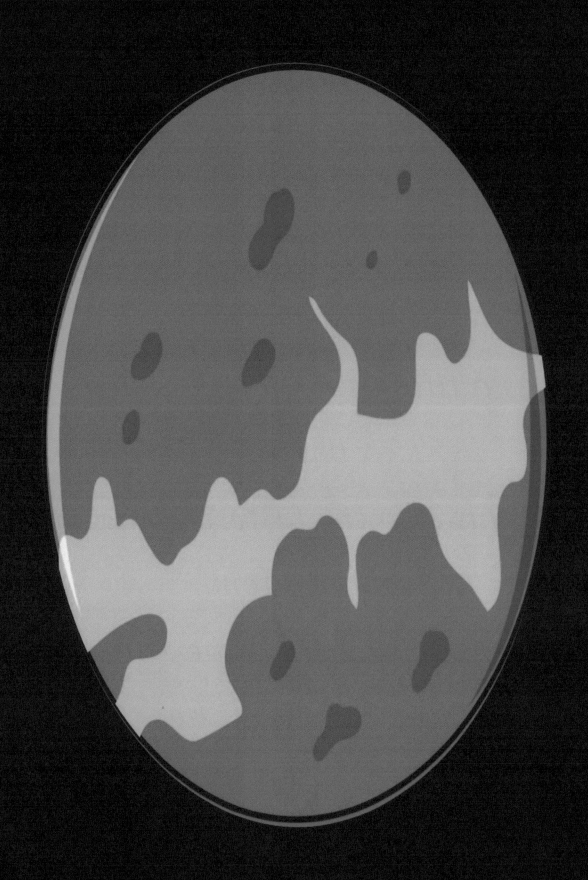

Venus

VENUS

Venus is the second closest planet to the Sun, and the closest to the Earth.

It is the hottest planet in the solar system.

Venus has a thick, toxic atmosphere, and yellowish clouds which smell like rotten eggs.

It rotates on its axis backward.

This means that on Venus, the Sun rises in the west and sets in the east.

This is opposite to what we experience on Earth.

Earth

EARTH

This is where we live!

Earth is the only planet known to be inhabited by living things.

If the Sun were as tall as a front door, Earth would be the size of a 20 pence coin.

It makes a complete orbit around the Sun in about 365 days, which is one year.

Earth's atmosphere is 78% nitrogen, 21% oxygen, and 1% of other substances which allow us to breathe and live.

Mars

MARS

Mars is the fourth planet from the Sun.

It is also known as the Red Planet.

It appears red because of the rusty iron

in the ground.

Mars is also a unique planet with

seasons, polar ice caps,

canyons, and extinct volcanoes.

It is one of the most explored bodies

in the solar system.

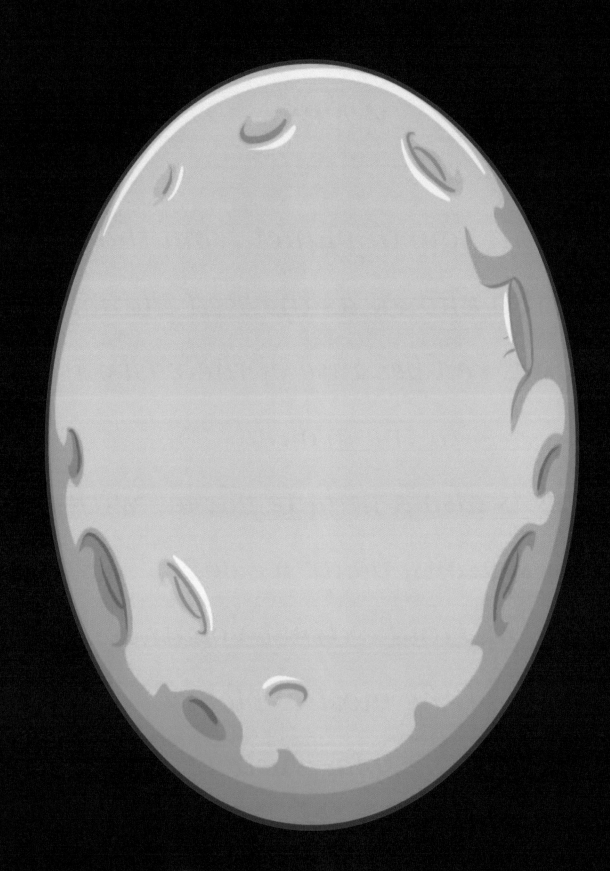

Jupiter

JUPITER

Jupiter is the biggest planet in the solar system; more than twice as big as all the other planets combined. If the Earth were the size of a grape, Jupiter would be slightly bigger than a football.

Jupiter contains gas, and doesn't have a solid surface. It has big storms like the Great Red Spot, which has been ongoing for hundreds of years.

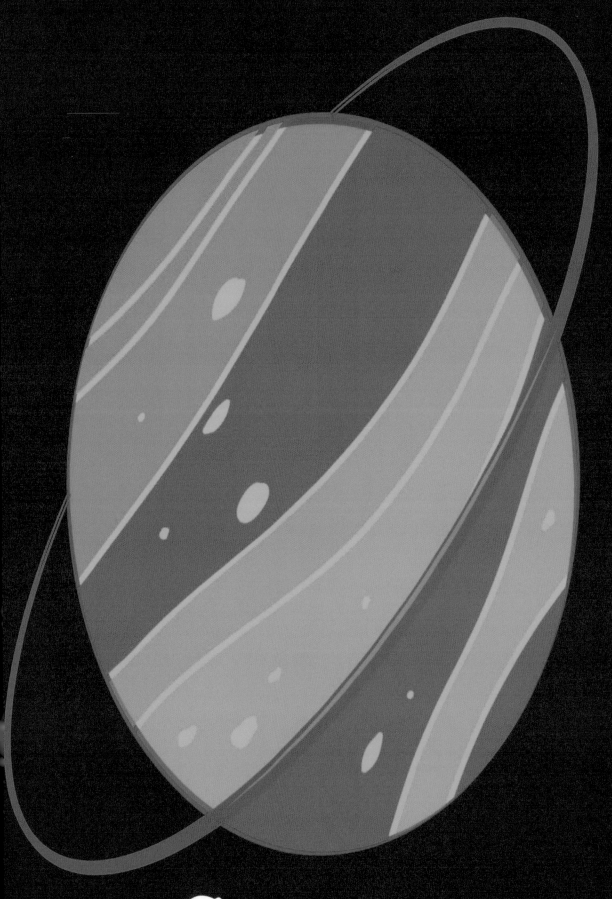

Saturn

SATURN

Saturn is the sixth planet from the Sun, and the second largest in the solar system.

Saturn has the most spectacular ring system, with seven rings which have gaps and divisions.

The rings contain chunks of ice and rocks.

Saturn is a gas planet, and therefore does not have a solid surface like the Earth.

Uranus

URANUS

Uranus is the seventh planet from the Sun.

It has inner rings which are narrow and dark, and outer rings which are brightly coloured and easier to see.

Like Venus, Uranus rotates from east to west, but it also rotates on its side.

Uranus contains water, methane, and ammonia fluids above a small rocky center.

Methane makes Uranus appear blue.

Neptune

NEPTUNE

Neptune is the eighth, and most distant planet in the solar system.

Neptune is dark, cold, and very windy.

It has rings which are clumps of dirt, and debris.

Neptune's atmosphere contains hydrogen[H2], helium[He], and methane.

The bluish appearance of Neptune is also due to methane.

Dr Fact: What have we learnt today?

Erin and Mo: There are eight planets in the solar system; Mercury, Venus, Earth, Mars, Jupiter, Saturn, Uranus, and Neptune!

Dr Fact: That is fantastic, well-done Erin and Mo.

Erin and Mo: Thank you, Dr Fact. See you next time.

Dr Fact: See you next time, Erin and Mo!

Questions

1. Which is the smallest planet in the solar system?

2. Which is the biggest planet in the solar system?

3. Which is the only planet inhabited by living things?

4. Which planets appear blue?

5. What substance gives them this blue appearance?

6. Which is the Red planet?

7. Which are the rocky planets?

Write your answers here

1.

2.

3.

4.

5.

6.

7.

Answers

1. Mercury

2. Jupiter

3. Earth

4. Uranus and Neptune

5. Methane

6. Mars

7. Mercury Venus, Earth, and Mars.

"Each of us has a unique part to play
in the healing of the world."
-Marianne Williamson

Printed in Poland
by Amazon Fulfillment
Poland Sp. z o.o., Wrocław